Can People
COUNT ON ME?
A Book about Responsibility

ROBIN NELSON

Lerner Publications Company • Minneapolis

Consultant:
Natasha Phillips, MA, Special Education
Special Education Teacher at Beadle
Elementary School
Yankton, South Dakota

Lerner Publications Company
A division of Lerner Publishing Group, Inc.
241 First Avenue North
Minneapolis, MN 55401 U.S.A.

For reading levels and more information, look up this title
at www.lernerbooks.com.

Library of Congress Cataloging-in-Publication Data

Nelson, Robin, 1971–
    Can people count on me? : a book about responsibility / Robin Nelson.
        pages   cm — (Show your character)
    Includes index.
    ISBN 978–1–4677–1363–4 (lib. bdg. : alk. paper)
    ISBN 978–1–4677–2521–7 (eBook)
    1. Personality development—Juvenile literature. 2. Responsibility—
Juvenile literature. I. Title.
BF723.P4N3945 2014
155.4'125—dc23   2013018367

Manufactured in the United States of America
1 – MG – 12/31/13

TABLE OF CONTENTS

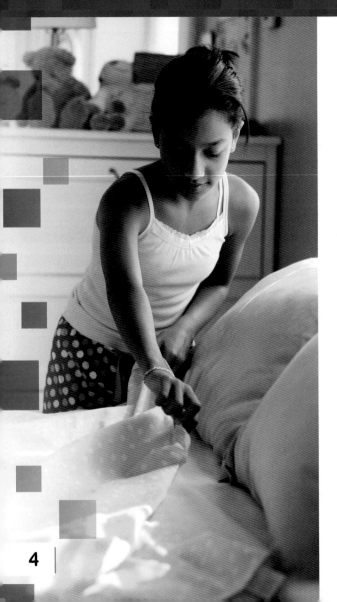

Do you clean your room when your mom asks? Do you return toys you borrowed? How often do you remember to walk your dog? Being **responsible** shows people they can count on you.

Being responsible means you do your jobs without being told. It means you keep promises. Someone who is responsible can be trusted.

Sometimes it's hard to be responsible. But when people know they can count on you, it makes everyone feel good. How can you be responsible? Let's look at some **questions and answers** about responsibility and find out!

I forgot to do my math worksheet last night. I started playing and forgot all about it. **HOW CAN I REMEMBER TO DO MY HOMEWORK?**

Homework is a big responsibility. It helps you learn. Your teacher is counting on you to do it. But it's hard to remember homework when there are so many other things to do.

Try doing your homework at the same time each day. Clean out your backpack when you get home, and then **just get that homework done**! You'll be happy to be finished and have the rest of the night to play.

Did You Know?

Writing down your assignments in a special notebook you keep in your backpack is a good way to remember what homework you need to do each night.

Write down your assignments to stay organized.

I return my library books when they are due. **AM I BEING RESPONSIBLE?**

Yes!
Returning library books is a great way to show you're responsible. When you borrow a library book, the librarian is counting on you to return it on or before the due date. That way others can check it out.

The librarian is also counting on you to **take care of the books you borrow**. Keep them in a safe place at home so they won't get damaged or lost.

It's no fun to be in band but never get to play! You need to remember your trumpet. Your parents might be able to remind you, but it's not their job. **You need to take responsibility.**

Every Monday night, put your trumpet next to the door. Then when you are walking out on Tuesday morning, you won't miss it.

My neighbor is going on vacation. He asked me to pick up his mail.

HOW CAN I SHOW MY NEIGHBOR HE CAN COUNT ON ME?

Decide on a time to get the mail each day. Set an alarm to remind yourself.

Keep your neighbor's mail in a safe spot at home. Put it in a bag or a basket.

When your neighbor is back, **bring him his mail as soon as you can.** When he sees how responsible you have been, he will know he can count on you next time.

I want a cat. My dad says I have to be responsible and take care of it. HOW CAN I PROVE I'M RESPONSIBLE ENOUGH FOR A PET?

Having a cat comes with many responsibilities. You have to feed it, clean its litter box, and take it to the vet. Before you get a cat, find out as much as you can about cats.

Read books to learn more about caring for a cat.

Read books about them. Talk to friends who have cats. Tell your dad everything you've learned and promise to take care of your cat.

When you bring your new cat home, **keep your promise**! Don't leave your pet's care up to your parents.

When we were walking home from the park, my friend threw her juice box in the grass. I told her that's littering. She said that someone else will pick it up. That doesn't seem right.

HOW CAN I SHOW MY FRIEND THAT LITTERING IS WRONG?

Good for you for wanting to be responsible! You're right—**it's not okay to litter.** We are all responsible for taking care of Earth. And we are responsible for our own actions. Tell your friend we all need to pitch in and take care of our planet. Ask her to pick up her juice box.

Did You Know?
Another way to be responsible is to recycle things like aluminum cans and newspapers.

You can recycle cans, newspapers, and plastic bottles.

What if she still won't pick it up?

Sometimes asking a friend to do something doesn't go smoothly. Your friend still might not pick up her juice box, even if you explain why it's important. In that case, the responsible thing to do is to **pick up the juice box yourself** and throw it away. You could even tell your friend you feel bad about seeing her litter because it hurts Earth. That might help her see why littering is wrong.

Sometimes people learn more from your actions than your words.

You can help Earth by volunteering to pick up litter in your city.

I walked home from school with Amy. She invited me to her house for a snack. When I got home, my mom was mad because she didn't know where I was.

WHAT SHOULD I HAVE DONE DIFFERENTLY?

Your mom was mad because she was worried when you didn't come home. You should have called to tell her where you were.

Take responsibility for your actions and apologize to your mom. Don't make excuses or blame anyone else. Then promise to call next time. And next time, **don't forget!**

Make sure a parent knows where you are at all times. Call if your plans change.

My brother and I made a fort with pillows and blankets. Then he got bored and went to do something else. I know I shouldn't leave the living room a mess.

HOW CAN I SHOW MY MOM I'M RESPONSIBLE?

Take responsibility for the mess. **Pick it up.**

You can ask your brother to help. But he might not help. If not, do the best you can on your own. Then next time he wants to play, tell him you'll play only if he helps clean up.

Take responsibility! Tell your mom you broke the vase.

She might be mad or disappointed at first, but your mom will also be **proud of your honesty.** She'll know she can count on you.

My dad asked me to water the plants outside. When I went outside, my neighbor asked if I wanted to ride bikes with her. I really want to play.

WHAT'S THE RIGHT THING TO DO?

Water the plants first. Your dad is counting on you. (And so are the thirsty flowers!) You could even ask your neighbor to help.

When your job is done, **then go play**. You'll enjoy playing more once you've done what you were supposed to!

MAKE A CHORE CHART

One way to show you are responsible is to do your chores at home. If you don't have specific chores, you can help your family by doing things like picking up your toys or putting dirty dishes in the dishwasher. A chore chart will help you remember which tasks you need to do. Just list the days of the week at the top. Then list your chores or other jobs you want to do on the side. Every time you do a chore, put a star sticker in the box for that chore on that day. Check out the chore chart on the next page for an example.

Chore	Sunday	Monday	Tuesday	Wednesday	Thursday	Friday	Saturday
Pick up my toys	★	★	★				
Put my dirty dishes in the dishwasher or sink	★	★	★				
Make my bed	★	★	★				
Put my laundry in the hamper	★	★	★				

alarm: a bell or other type of sound that prompts you to do something

apologize: to say you are sorry

borrow: to take and use something before returning it

damaged: broken or ripped

librarian: a person who is specially trained to work in a library

littering: leaving trash on the ground

proud: happy because of something you did

responsible: a word to describe someone who can be trusted to do what is right

trumpet: a musical instrument that you blow into. A trumpet has three buttons that you press to make different notes.

vet: an animal doctor. *Vet* is short for *veterinarian.*

FURTHER INFORMATION

Bullard, Lisa. *Rally for Recycling*. Minneapolis: Millbrook Press, 2012.
Discover how to reduce, reuse, and recycle, and take responsibility for planet Earth.

Espeland, Pamela. *Knowing and Doing What's Right: The Positive Values Assets*. Minneapolis: Free Spirit Publishing, 2006.
Learn simple, everyday ways you can make good choices and build positive character assets.

Nelson, Robin. *How I Clean My Room*. Minneapolis: Lerner Publications, 2014.
Follow along in this fun, simple read as a child shows one way to be responsible.

"The Responsibility Rap"
http://www.youtube.com/watch?v=UOuvJMibfVo&feature=related
"The Responsibility Rap" is featured in the Buckalope Elementary puppet video series, which explores character.

INDEX

PHOTO ACKNOWLEDGMENTS

The images in this book are used with the permission of: © KidStock/Blend Images/Getty Images, p. 4; © iStockphoto.com/sonyae, p. 5; © Little Blue Wolf Productions/Royalty-Free/CORBIS, p. 6; © Stockbyte, p. 7; © Jeffrey Coolidge/Royalty-Free/CORBIS, p. 8; © iStockphoto.com/asiseeit, pp. 9, 20; © iStockphoto.com/CEFutcher, p. 10; © iStockphoto.com/yenwen, p. 11; © iStockphoto.com/Juanmonino, p. 13; © iStockphoto.com/Fertnig, p. 14; © Stock Connection/SuperStock, p. 15; © Diana Haronis dianasphotoart.com/Flickr/Getty Images, p. 16; © iStockphoto.com/Kais Tolmats, p. 17; © iStockphoto.com/charlybutcher, p. 18; © Fuse/Getty Images, p. 19; © iStockphoto.com/LattaPictures, p. 21; © Adam Gault/OJO Images/Getty Images, p. 24; © Rob Lewine/Getty Images, p. 25 © Smit/Shutterstock.com, pp. 26, 27.

Front Cover: © Xavier Gallego Morell/Dreamstime.com.

Main body text set in ChurchwardSamoa Regular. Typeface provided by Chank.